I0762521
WHOHQ

**To Lesya Nirschl—music is important—EL**

**To my father, who filled my childhood with the sound of the Beatles—FL**

PENGUIN WORKSHOP
An imprint of Penguin Random House LLC
1745 Broadway, New York, NY 10019
penguinrandomhouse.com

Copyright © 2026 by Penguin Random House LLC

Penguin Random House values and supports copyright. Copyright fuels creativity, encourages diverse voices, promotes free speech, and creates a vibrant culture. Thank you for buying an authorized edition of this book and for complying with copyright laws by not reproducing, scanning, or distributing any part of it in any form without permission. You are supporting writers and allowing Penguin Random House to continue to publish books for every reader. Please note that no part of this book may be used or reproduced in any manner for the purpose of training artificial intelligence technologies or systems.

PENGUIN is a registered trademark and PENGUIN WORKSHOP is a trademark of Penguin Books Ltd.
WHO HQ & Design is a registered trademark of Penguin Random House LLC.

Design by Taylor Abatiell
Text set in Adobe Garamond Pro

The art was created using Adobe Photoshop.

Library of Congress Cataloging-in-Publication Data is available.

First published in the United States of America by Penguin Workshop, 2026

Manufactured in China
HH

ISBN 9798217053520
10 9 8 7 6 5 4 3 2 1

The authorized representative in the EU for product safety and compliance is Penguin Random House Ireland, Morrison Chambers, 32 Nassau Street, Dublin D02 YH68, Ireland, https://eu-contact.penguin.ie.

**A WHO HQ ILLUSTRATED BIOGRAPHY**

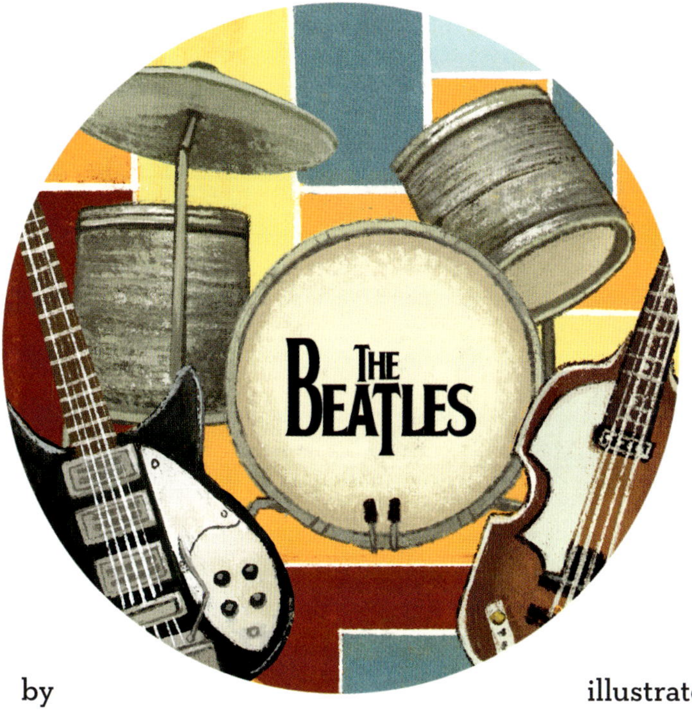

by
Ellen Labrecque

illustrated by
Fanny Liem

Penguin Workshop

Four young musicians with "mop top" hair stood onstage in black suits. It was February 9, 1964, and a new British band was appearing on *The Ed Sullivan Show* in New York City. This was a variety show that showcased all kinds of talented performers. More than seventy-three million people watched the band on television. The teenagers in the studio audience shrieked and screamed in delight.

**Who were these four musicians?**

The Beatles are the greatest, most famous, and most influential rock and roll band of all time. All four members of the band came from the same working-class city: Liverpool, England.

John Lennon was a lead singer and guitar player. He and the band's drummer, Richard Starkey, known as Ringo Starr, were the oldest. They were both born in 1940. The other lead singer and guitar player, Paul McCartney, was born in 1942. George Harrison, singer and guitar player, was the youngest, born in 1943.

John Lennon was born to Julia and Alfred. Alfred worked on a ship and was gone for months at a time. Julia loved her son but could not take care of him. Instead, John was raised by his Aunt Mimi and Uncle George. He was a creative kid who loved art and music. When he was around fifteen, John formed a band called the Quarrymen. The band was named after John's high school, Quarry Bank.

Paul McCartney's parents were named Jim and Mary. Jim was a cotton salesman who had played piano in a jazz band. Paul's mom was a nurse. One day, Paul's dad gave him a trumpet. But Paul wanted to sing at the same time, so he swapped it for a guitar! Paul was hooked and practiced a lot.

In the summer of 1957, when Paul was fifteen, he went to see the Quarrymen play at a local church. He met John and performed some songs for him. John was impressed! Soon after, Paul joined John's band.

George Harrison's mom, Louise, taught ballroom dancing, and his dad, Harold, drove a bus. When George was thirteen, he became interested in music, especially rock and roll. His mom bought him a guitar. He practiced so much, he made his fingers bleed. At about the same time, George met Paul while riding on a bus. As they talked, they realized they shared the same love of music. Paul eventually invited George to join the Quarrymen, too.

Ringo Starr was the oldest of the Beatles and the last to join the band. Ringo was named Richard Starkey after his dad. His mom's name was Elsie. Ringo was sick a lot as a kid. He had long stays in the hospital. A music teacher visited the sick children to keep them entertained. Ringo learned to play the drums in the hospital. "When I was thirteen, I only wanted to be a drummer," he said.

In 1960, the Quarrymen changed the band's name to the Beatles. John Lennon liked that their new name had a double meaning. "When you said it, people thought of crawly things," John explained. "And when you read it, it was beat music."

The band soon booked a gig at a club in Hamburg, Germany, starting in 1960. They played there for a few months at a time, sometimes for six or more hours a night. When they returned to Liverpool and started playing shows there, a local businessman named Brian Epstein saw them. He thought they were awesome and offered to help them become much more famous. Brian became the band's manager.

Brian did two important things for the band right away. First, he told them to start dressing in identical suits. Brian thought it made the band look more professional. The suits "made us one person, like a four-headed monster," Paul explained. Brian also helped them replace their current drummer, Pete Best, with a new drummer, Ringo Starr.

Ringo played in another band at the time. John, Paul, and George knew he was talented. Ringo officially joined the Beatles on August 18, 1962.

**The four would soon be known as the "Fab Four." The "fab" was short for fabulous.**

The Beatles were not just singers and musicians. They were great songwriters—especially Paul and John. They wrote songs that had snappy lyrics and, of course, strong beats! Fans could easily sing and dance along with them. The four young men were handsome and had a funny, cool way about them. "The Beatles were kind of the dream of how you might be with your friends as you went through life," said movie writer and fan Richard Curtis.

As the Beatles sang in clubs in England, they became more and more popular. In March 1963, they put out their first album in the United Kingdom, *Please Please Me*. It was a smash hit. The band became so famous that fans shrieked and chased after them wherever they went. A newspaper in London called this fan enthusiasm "Beatlemania."

One of the Beatles' most popular songs was called "I Want to Hold Your Hand." It was so simple but so catchy! The Beatles had not performed in the United States yet. But this song was played on the radio there a lot. In February 1964, it topped the charts, and the Beatles arrived in New York City to perform on *The Ed Sullivan Show*.

When the Beatles arrived in New York City, mobs of fans greeted them at the airport. Young girls fainted and cried when they saw them. The four musicians answered journalists' questions at the airport. They were charming, funny, and bold. Their fans loved them even more. Their performance on *The Ed Sullivan Show* was the beginning of the British Invasion, when British bands and actors became popular in America, too.

The Beatles toured all over the world. They performed in front of giant crowds, sometimes as many as fifty thousand people. Their performances were amazing but also exhausting. The fans screamed so loudly that the Beatles could not hear their own music. When on tour, they could not go out in public because fans mobbed them. One time at a concert in Seattle, Washington, they had to escape fans by hiding in an ambulance.

Although the Beatles loved being loved, it became too much. They were weary of the suffocating fan attention. "We became trapped," George said. On August 29, 1966, the Beatles performed in front of twenty-five thousand fans in San Francisco, California. Before the show, Paul said to a friend, "Don't tell anyone, but this is probably our last gig." **And . . . it was.**

The Beatles were done with performing live, but they still made music together. They spent all their time in their London studio working on new songs. Paul and John were the creative engines of the band. Two songs, one called "Strawberry Fields Forever" and one called "Penny Lane," were touching tunes that looked back at their time growing up in Liverpool. In 1967, the Beatles released the album *Sgt. Pepper's Lonely Hearts Club Band*, which sounded very different. A lot of unique instruments, like the Indian sitar, were used. The songs had a groovy tone.

# Beatles Albums

The Beatles are the bestselling band of all time. They have sold more than five hundred million albums! They released twelve albums in the United Kingdom from 1963 to 1970. They are:

*Please Please Me*
1963

*With the Beatles*
1963

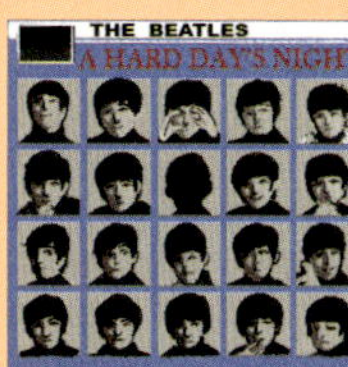


*A Hard Day's Night*
1964

*Beatles for Sale*
1964

*Help!*
1965

*Rubber Soul*
1965

*Revolver*
1966

*Sgt. Pepper's Lonely Hearts Club Band*
1967

*The Beatles*
(also called
*The White Album*)
1968

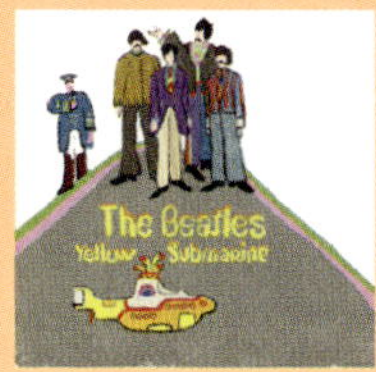


*Yellow Submarine*
1969

*Abbey Road*
1969

*Let It Be*
1970

The Beatles' fashion had also changed. They didn't dress in the same suits anymore. Instead, they looked different from their younger selves, as well as from each other. All of them grew their hair long, and sometimes they had mustaches or beards. They wore bright and bold colors. They dressed in the style of the time—like hippies.

In January 1969, the Beatles started their next big project, an album and documentary called *Let It Be*. It ended up being a big mess. After almost ten years together, the band members were simply tired of one another. They picked fights and didn't want to listen to each other's ideas. George and John talked about leaving the Beatles.

# The 1960s

The 1960s was a decade filled with change, creativity, peace, and love. People fought for equality for all Americans, especially Black Americans. Humans walked on the moon for the first time!

In music, rock and roll was played constantly on the radio. A music festival was held near Woodstock, New York, in August 1969. The festival became a symbol of the whole decade. Hundreds of thousands came to Woodstock to hear famous bands and also to promote peace and love. Many hippies were there. Hippies were people who wore bright, flowy, colorful clothing and usually grew their hair long. They wanted to make the world a better place by spreading kindness and ending all war. The Beatles, who identified with hippies, wanted to do these things, too.

Paul was the saddest about the direction the band was going. He convinced the Beatles to do another studio album. They called it *Abbey Road*, which was the street that their recording studio was on in London. Despite the hopeful lyrics in the song "Here Comes the Sun," the Beatles were not all right. They were going to break up.

*Abbey Road* was a big hit. It didn't matter. The Beatles were no longer a band by 1970. There were many reasons why, but mostly each member wanted to try things on his own. George was a talented songwriter and wanted more chances to prove this. Paul was ready for a solo career. Ringo was tired of the band fighting. John wanted to spend more time with his new wife, artist Yoko Ono.

# After the Beatles

## John Lennon

(1940–1980)

John and Yoko Ono were anti-war activists. John wrote anti-war songs and appeared at events to promote world peace. In 1971, John released his solo album *Imagine*. Despite the title song's anti-violence message, John was shot and killed by an angry fan in 1980, when he was forty years old.

## Paul McCartney

(1942–)

Paul became the most successful solo artist of the four Beatles. Since the breakup of the Beatles, Paul has released more than twenty studio records that include nine number one hits on the *Billboard* Hot 100 chart. He has won nineteen Grammy Awards and was knighted by the queen of England in 1997.

## George Harrison

(1943–2001)

George explored his interest in Indian music. He also spent a lot of time participating in concerts that raised money for charities. George released his first solo album, *All Things Must Pass*, in 1970. The song "My Sweet Lord" was his most popular song of his solo work. George died of cancer when he was fifty-eight years old.

## Ringo Starr

(1940–)

Ringo continued to perform and produce music. In 1989, he became the leader of Ringo Starr and His All-Starr Band, a collection of different rock and roll musicians who'd come together to perform their greatest hits. Ringo recorded several hits, but he became just as well-known for his speaking voice. He was the narrator for the Thomas the Tank Engine television series! Ringo was knighted by the Duke of Cambridge in 2018.

The Beatles were together for just ten years—but their impact is forever. "We were the biggest band in the land," Ringo said. Their song "Yesterday" is one of their most famous. It is about missing someone you loved who is now gone. Fans of all ages will forever love the Beatles of yesterday.

***Yet their music — and all they meant to the world — will continue to be deeply powerful today, tomorrow, and into the future.***

# Bibliography

***Books for young readers**


The Beatles. ***The Beatles Anthology***. San Francisco: Chronicle Books, 2000.

Burrows, Terry. ***The Beatles: The Complete Illustrated Story***. London: Carlton, 1996.

*Cooper, Ilene. ***This Boy: The Early Lives of John Lennon and Paul McCartney***. New York: Viking, 2023.

Davies, Hunter. ***The Beatles***. 2nd revised edition. New York: W. W. Norton and Company, 2004.

*Edgers, Geoff. ***Who Were the Beatles?*** New York: Penguin Workshop, 2006.

Howard, Ron, director. ***The Beatles: Eight Days a Week—The Touring Years***. London: Apple Corps Limited, 2016.

Lewisohn, Mark. ***Tune In***. Volume 1 of ***The Beatles: All These Years***. New York: Crown Archetype, 2013.

Spitz, Bob. ***The Beatles: The Biography***. New York: Little, Brown, 2005.

# Timeline

1940 — Richard Starkey (Ringo Starr) is born on July 7

— John Lennon is born on October 9

1942 — Paul McCartney is born on June 18

1943 — George Harrison is born on February 25

1956 — John Lennon forms a band called the Quarrymen

1957 — Paul McCartney joins the Quarrymen

1958 — George Harrison joins the Quarrymen

1960 — The Quarrymen change their name to the Beatles

1962 — Ringo Starr joins the band as their new drummer

The Beatles release their first album, *Please Please Me* — **1963**

On February 9, the Beatles appear on *The Ed Sullivan Show* — **1964**

The song "Yesterday" becomes a number one hit — **1965**

The Beatles play their last concert — **1966**

*Sgt. Pepper's Lonely Hearts Club Band* is released — **1967**

The Beatles have officially broken up — **1970**

John Lennon dies — **1980**

George Harrison dies — **2001**

In December, Paul McCartney and Ringo Starr reunite to perform onstage at a show in London — **2024**

WHOHQ
WHOHQ
WHOHQ
WHOHQ
WHOHQ
WHOHQ
WHOHQ
WHOHQ
WHOHQ